INTRODUCTION

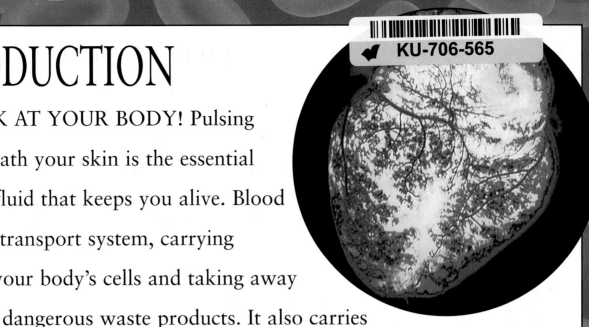

LOOK AT YOUR BODY! Pulsing beneath your skin is the essential red fluid that keeps you alive. Blood is the body's transport system, carrying nutrients to your body's cells and taking away dangerous waste products. It also carries your body's chemical messengers, hormones, which regulate many of your functions.

Blood plays a vital role in defending your body from foreign invaders, such as germs. It seals up many wounds that might occur, and its own silent guardians patrol every nook and cranny of your body, ready to gobble up anything that may threaten your well-being.

Every minute of every day, this vital red liquid flows endlessly around your body, pushed by the rhythmic pumping of your heart.

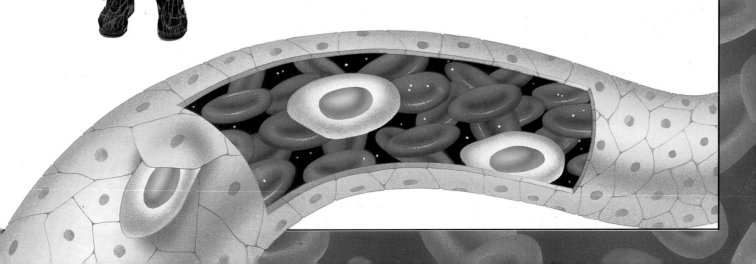

NOT ALL BLOOD *is* RED

W E SOMETIMES SEE OUR OWN BLOOD, when we are scratched or cut. Like a lot of other animals, including birds, fish and amphibians, the blood that oozes out of a wound is red. However, not all blood in the animal kingdom is this colour. Some animals have blue or even clear blood, while others may have no blood at all!

The differences between human and animal blood systems do not end there. Nature has developed a wide range of methods, according to the needs of an animal, which pass nutrients around a body and remove its waste products.

HOW MANY HEARTS?
An earthworm (above) has 10 hearts. These are found near the front of the worm. They lie in pairs down the sides of the body. Each heart is simply a bulge in one of the main blood vessels. They squeeze or pulse slowly to push the blood around.

4

NO BLOOD
Very simple creatures, like sea anemones (left), do not have a proper blood system with a heart, blood vessels and blood. As the anemone digests its food, nutrients simply seep out of the stomach chamber. From there, nutrients pass into and through its body, with its fluid-filled chambers and soft, jelly-like parts.

BIG HEARTED
Bigger animals usually have bigger hearts. The biggest animals in the world are the great whales, such as the blue whale (below). They also have the largest hearts of any animals. Being an air-breathing, warm-blooded mammal like you, the blue whale's heart has almost exactly the same structure as a human heart. However, it is about the size of a small car and weighs as much as eight adult humans!

LOOK AT YOUR BODY

BLOOD

STEVE PARKER

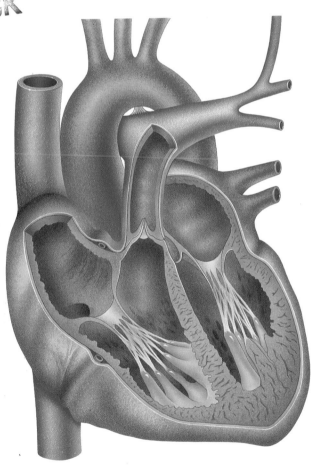

Franklin Watts
London • Sydney

This edition published in 2001
© Aladdin Books Ltd 1997

All rights reserved Designed and produced by Aladdin Books Ltd 28 Percy Street London W1P 0LD

First published in Great Britain in 1997 by Franklin Watts 96 Leonard Street London EC2A 4XD

ISBN 0 7496 2791 3 (hbk)
ISBN 0 7496 4110 X (pbk)

Printed in U.A.E.

Editor
Jon Richards

Design
David West
Children's Book Design
Designer Robert Perry
Illustrators
Ian Thompson
& Mark Iley

Picture Research
Brooks Krikler Research
Consultant
Dr Rachel Levene MB.BS, DCH, DRCOG

Steve Parker has written over 100 books for children, many of these concerning human anatomy and physiology.

CONTENTS

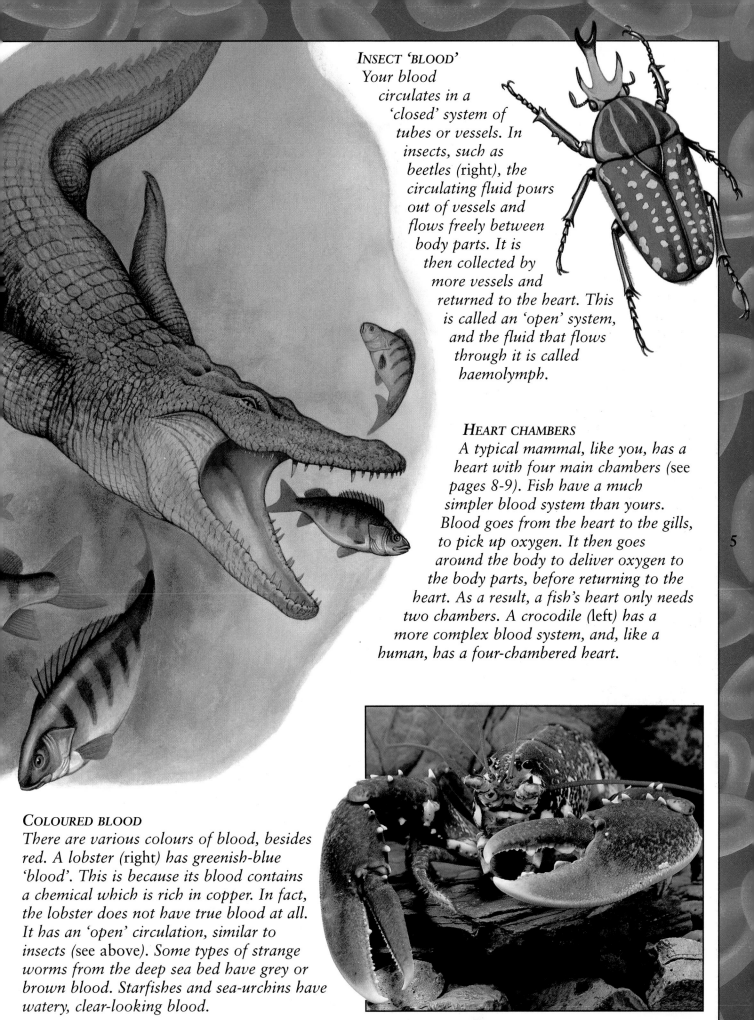

INSECT 'BLOOD'

Your blood circulates in a 'closed' system of tubes or vessels. In insects, such as beetles (right), the circulating fluid pours out of vessels and flows freely between body parts. It is then collected by more vessels and returned to the heart. This is called an 'open' system, and the fluid that flows through it is called haemolymph.

HEART CHAMBERS

A typical mammal, like you, has a heart with four main chambers (see pages 8-9). Fish have a much simpler blood system than yours. Blood goes from the heart to the gills, to pick up oxygen. It then goes around the body to deliver oxygen to the body parts, before returning to the heart. As a result, a fish's heart only needs two chambers. A crocodile (left) has a more complex blood system, and, like a human, has a four-chambered heart.

COLOURED BLOOD

There are various colours of blood, besides red. A lobster (right) has greenish-blue 'blood'. This is because its blood contains a chemical which is rich in copper. In fact, the lobster does not have true blood at all. It has an 'open' circulation, similar to insects (see above). Some types of strange worms from the deep sea bed have grey or brown blood. Starfishes and sea-urchins have watery, clear-looking blood.

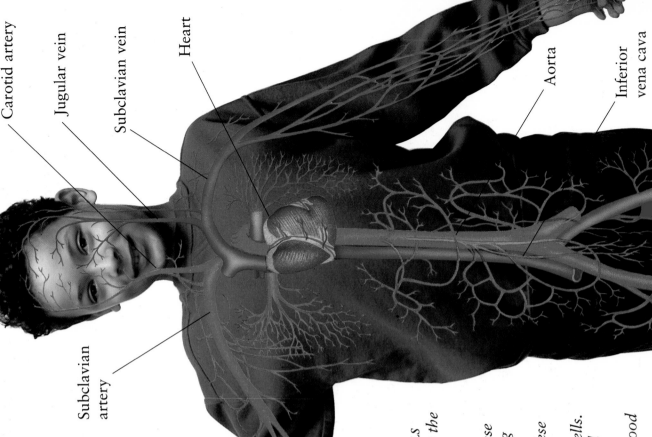

The BLOODSTREAM

BLOOD IS PUMPED by your heart through a network of tubes, called blood vessels. This network carries blood to all parts of your body, from the very top of your head to the tips of your toes (*right*). Every single cell receives its requirement of nutrients, carried to them by the red liquid.

This network of vessels is called the circulatory system because the blood circulates, or flows endlessly around. The flow of blood is called the bloodstream.

Carotid artery

Jugular vein

Subclavian vein

Heart

Aorta

Inferior vena cava

Subclavian artery

*MAIN TYPES OF BLOOD VESSELS
Not all the blood vessels are the same. The wide vessels that carry blood away from the heart are called arteries. These divide many times, becoming smaller, until they are tiny vessels called capillaries. These form a fine mesh of blood vessels between the body's cells. The capillaries then join and merge to form wide vessels, called veins, that take the blood back to the heart (left).*

Veins

Capillaries

Arteries

Femoral artery

Femoral vein

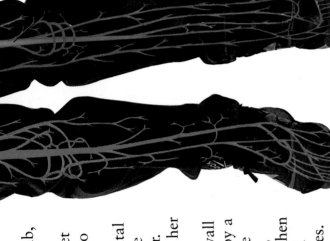

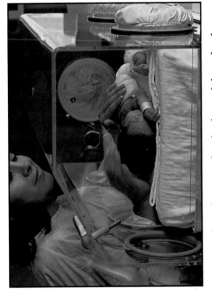

Inside its mother's womb, a baby cannot breathe air to get oxygen, or eat to get nutrients. Instead, these vital substances come from the mother. They pass from her blood into the baby's blood, through a specialized organ called the placenta. This is embedded in the wall of the womb. The baby is attached to the placenta by a rope-like part called the umbilical cord. At birth, the baby can breathe and feed for itself. Because of this, the baby's heart and blood system change slightly when it is born. Blood is diverted away from the cord and placenta, towards the baby's own lungs and intestines.

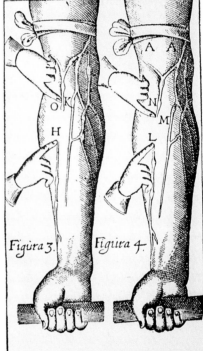

Figura 3.   Figura 4.

WILLIAM HARVEY
In ancient times, people did not understand how blood got around the body. They thought that blood was continually formed in certain parts, such as the lungs, and that it ebbed and flowed, to and fro in the vessels with each heart-beat. English doctor William

Harvey carried out simple experiments to prove that the blood actually circulated around the body in one direction (above). His book of 1628 showed that small valves in some of the blood vessels stopped the blood from flowing backwards (see pages 12-13).

HEART DEVELOPMENT
In the unborn baby, the heart begins as thicker regions of two tiny tubes. These develop about 21 days after fertilization (left). They merge and twist, and as some parts thicken, others become thinner, and folds form. By five weeks, the heart has its four-chambered structure and is pumping blood around the tiny body.

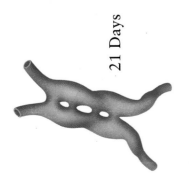

21 Days

23 Days

32 Days

7

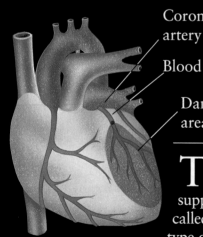

Superior vena cava

Aorta

LEFT ATRIUM

RIGHT ATRIUM

LEFT VENTRICLE

RIGHT VENTRICLE

HEART AND MAIN VESSELS
The vessels that carry blood into and out of the heart are the largest in the body. Blood enters the right side of the heart through two veins, called the inferior vena cava and the superior vena cava (right). Blood leaves the heart's left side through the aorta. This arches over the top of the heart before going down the middle of the body (above).

Inferior vena cava

Coronary artery

Blood clot

Damaged area

The heart is a very strong part of the body, with a blood supply brought by its own vessels, called coronary arteries. In one type of heart attack, a blood clot gets wedged in a coronary artery and blocks the blood flow. The area of the heart's muscle supplied with blood by this artery becomes damaged. It may cause heart pain, interfere with the heart's beating or stop it altogether. The blockage can be seen on an angiogram – an X-ray image produced by injecting a dye which shows up under X-rays (*right*).

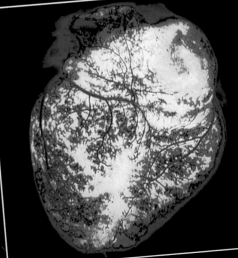

The HEART

THE HEART IS, IN FACT, two pumps, with two sets of pumping chambers side by side. Each set consists of a small upper chamber, called the atrium, and a larger lower chamber, called the ventricle. Blood from the main veins goes into the atria and then into the ventricles. The ventricles have thick walls of muscle. This muscle contracts powerfully to squeeze blood out of the heart. The blood then enters the arteries which carry it around the body, before it returns to the heart (*see* pages 10-11).

REPLACEMENT HEARTS

There are various treatments for heart disease. One option is to use a donated human heart to replace the diseased one. In the future, donated hearts may come from animals, such as pigs. Alternatively, the whole heart can be replaced by a mechanical, artificial heart (above).

POSITION OF THE HEART

The heart sits in the front of your chest, almost surrounded by the two lungs (right). It is slightly to your left side, with its right side behind the breastbone. The bottom of the left ventricle forms the heart's lowest pointed part. This is tilted diagonally to the left and downwards.

The heart's beating motions can be felt just below your fifth left rib, about one palm's width from the middle of the body. Above the heart is the tangle of the main blood vessels. Directly below is the main dome-shaped breathing muscle, the diaphragm. This forms the floor of your chest.

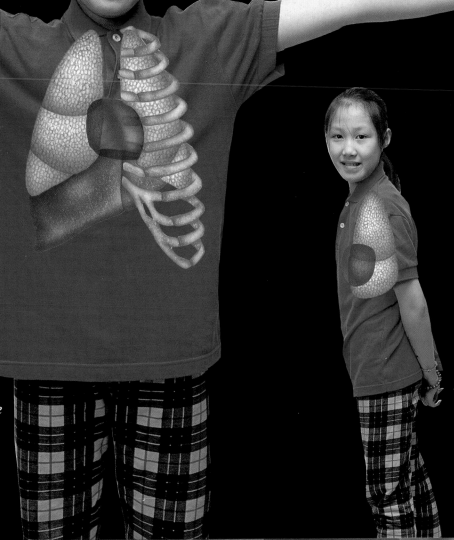

TRANSPLANTATION
TEXAS HEART INSTITUTE

HOW *the* HEART BEATS

EACH TIME YOUR HEART BEATS, the muscles in the walls of the heart relax to take blood in from the veins and then contract to push it out again. The muscle tissue is much stronger in the lower chambers, the ventricles. This is because they have to push the blood out of the heart with great force. Each beat of the heart usually takes about a second before it is repeated. This ensures that blood is always flowing around your body. However, the rate at which the heart beats can increase or decrease, depending on your body's requirements.

CHANGING HEART RATE
Your level of activity can change the speed of your heart-beat. When you are asleep, your heart beats about 50-70 times per minute. If you are eating (above), this increases to 70-90 beats per minute, but if you are doing very hard exercise it can increase to nearly 200 beats per minute.

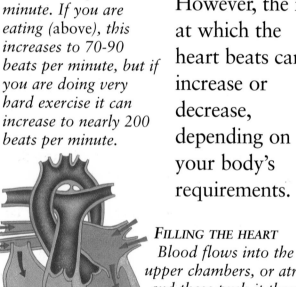

FILLING THE HEART
Blood flows into the upper chambers, or atria, and these push it through the valves into the lower chambers (left). At this time, blood pressure is at its lowest.

EMPTYING THE HEART
The lower chambers, or ventricles, contract powerfully. This forces blood out of the heart into the system of arteries (right). At this time, the force of the blood flow, called blood pressure, is at its highest.

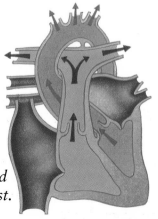

CONTROL VALVES
If the blood system had no valves, the blood would simply slosh around, instead of flowing through the blood vessels in one direction. Valves are found between the chambers of the heart and in the main veins.
These valves consist of tough but flexible pouches. When blood is being pushed along by the heart, the valves open to let blood flow the right way (above left). However, when the heart is filling and blood pressure drops, the valves shut, stopping the blood flowing the wrong way (above right). Damaged valves may not close properly and may have to be replaced (see page 28).

ALL A FLUTTER

In animals, the pulse rate depends partly on body size. Small creatures, like mice and shrews, have faster pulse rates than bigger ones, like elephants and whales. For example, an elephant's pulse rate is about 20-25 beats per minute. A human averages 60-80 per minute, while a canary's heart may beat over 300 times per minute (below).

In some cases of heart disease, the heart is unable to beat with a steady rhythm. If this happens, an artificial pacemaker (*below*) may be fitted. This is usually put under the skin of the shoulder (*above*) and connected to the heart by wires. The latest pacemakers have a microchip to vary the heart's rate according to the body's needs, and its batteries last many years.

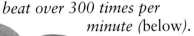

⊖ ⊕ **VS-1**
🌐 **Intermedics Inc.**
FREEPORT, TEXAS

COSMOS II
Model 284-05

DDD

FEEL THE RHYTHM

Each heart-beat is coordinated by tiny electrical signals in the heart's muscle tissue. The high-pressure surges of blood produced by each heart-beat make the walls of the arteries bulge (right), forming waves that travel away from the heart. These bulges can be felt as pulses where blood vessels run over a bone or hard surface. The most convenient place to feel the pulse is in the wrist. However, it can also be felt in the neck, the groin, the ankle and the top of the foot (left).

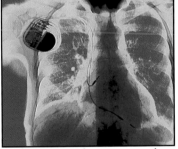

BLOOD VESSELS

THE THREE TYPES of blood vessels found in the blood system vary greatly in size and structure. This is because the vessels do different jobs. Arteries are wide and have thick walls, because they have to carry huge amounts of blood at very high pressure. Capillaries are tiny with very thin walls which allow nutrients to pass into the body's cells. Veins are wide, but have thinner walls than arteries because the pressure in them is much lower.

INSIDE A VESSEL
The space inside a blood vessel (above) gets smaller as the blood vessels divide. In capillaries the space is so small that only one blood cell at a time can pass through.

VEIN
The muscle layer in veins (left) is much thinner than in arteries. Veins also have valves to stop blood flowing the wrong way (see page 10).

CAPILLARY
A typical capillary is very short and far thinner than a human hair. Its walls are only one cell thick, so substances can pass through them (bottom).

VEIN

ARTERY

Muscle layer

ARTERY
The walls of arteries (right) contain thick layers of muscle. The space in the artery gets smaller when the muscle contracts and widens when it relaxes. This helps control blood flow around the body.

Capillary cross-section

Muscle layer

SIZE, SPEED AND PRESSURE

As blood flows away from the heart, the force or pressure at which it flows decreases (right). When it travels along the arteries it is being forced through at very high pressures. As the arteries divide into smaller and smaller vessels, so the pressure and the speed of blood flow drop. By the time the blood reaches the veins, blood pressure is at its lowest and the speed at which it travels is little more than a trickle. It then flows back into the heart to be forced out again at high pressure.

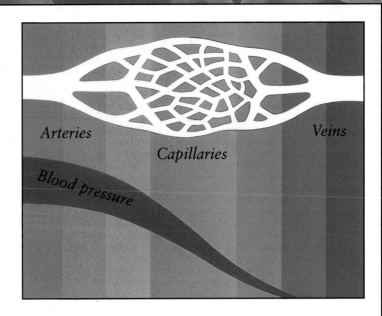

Arteries

Capillaries

Veins

Blood pressure

Doctors have developed a way of treating a blocked coronary artery (*see* page 8) by by-passing the blood vessel altogether. They remove a less important blood vessel, usually a vein from the leg (*left*). This vessel is then sewn onto the coronary artery on either side of the blockage (*right*). Blood that then flows to the coronary artery is re-routed along this transplanted vessel, avoiding the blockage and ensuring the heart's muscle gets all the nutrients it needs.

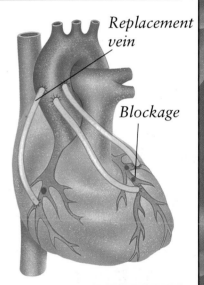

Replacement vein

Blockage

13

PASSING THROUGH WALLS

The thinness of the capillary walls is vital to the role that blood plays in carrying substances around the body. If the walls were any thicker, the blood would not be able to absorb oxygen from the lungs (right). Without oxygen, your body's cells would not be able to get energy from food. As a result, they would not be able to carry out any of their functions.

Similarly, thicker capillaries would prevent the absorption of wastes that your body's cells produce all the time. If these built up in your body, they could prove to be harmful.

Waste out

Oxygen in

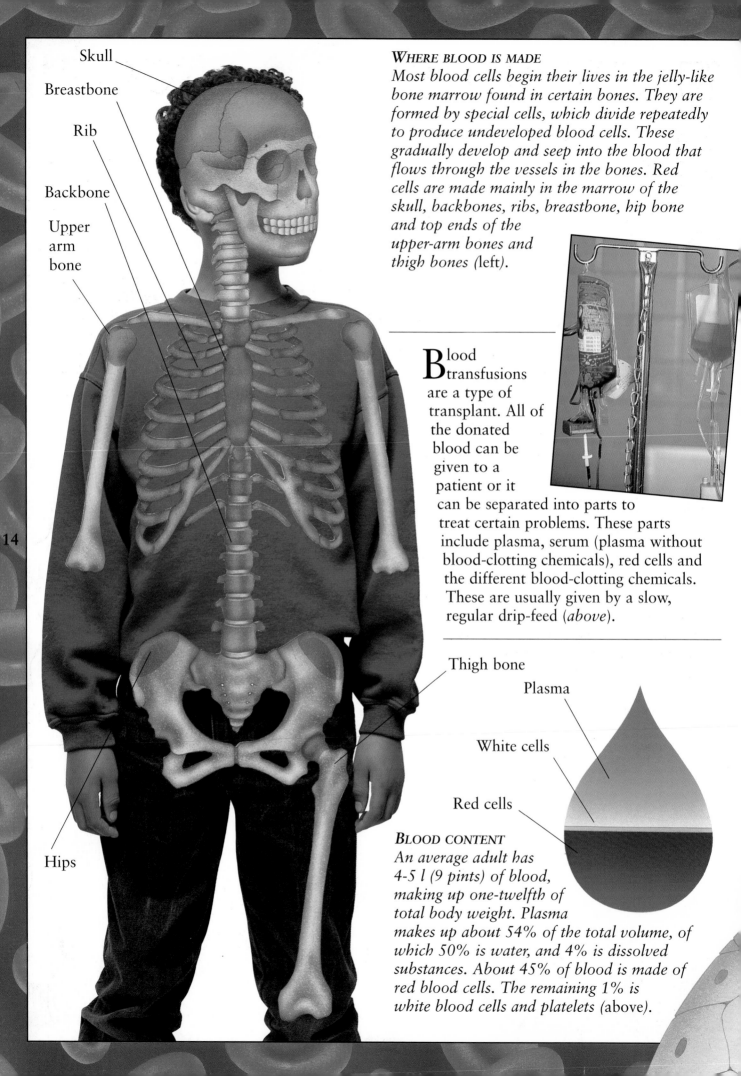

Skull

Breastbone

Rib

Backbone

Upper
arm
bone

Hips

Thigh bone

WHERE BLOOD IS MADE
Most blood cells begin their lives in the jelly-like bone marrow found in certain bones. They are formed by special cells, which divide repeatedly to produce undeveloped blood cells. These gradually develop and seep into the blood that flows through the vessels in the bones. Red cells are made mainly in the marrow of the skull, backbones, ribs, breastbone, hip bone and top ends of the upper-arm bones and thigh bones (left).

Blood transfusions are a type of transplant. All of the donated blood can be given to a patient or it can be separated into parts to treat certain problems. These parts include plasma, serum (plasma without blood-clotting chemicals), red cells and the different blood-clotting chemicals. These are usually given by a slow, regular drip-feed (*above*).

Plasma

White cells

Red cells

BLOOD CONTENT
An average adult has 4-5 l (9 pints) of blood, making up one-twelfth of total body weight. Plasma makes up about 54% of the total volume, of which 50% is water, and 4% is dissolved substances. About 45% of blood is made of red blood cells. The remaining 1% is white blood cells and platelets (above).

WHAT'S *in* BLOOD?

BLOOD IS MADE UP OF billions of tiny cells floating in a watery liquid. There are two main types of blood cells – red cells and white cells. Each cell has one main task. Red cells transport oxygen and white cells help to clean the blood and tissues. There are also tiny fragments called platelets. These are involved in blood clotting. The watery liquid is called plasma. It contains hundreds of substances, such as nutrients from digestion, blood-clotting chemicals, antibodies to attack germs, and chemical messengers, called hormones, that control the body's processes.

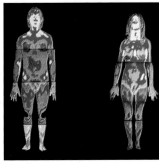

SPREADING HEAT
In addition to transporting chemicals and substances, blood also spreads out body heat (above). It carries warmth from hotter parts of the body to cooler parts. This keeps the body temperature around 36-37°C (97-99°F).

15

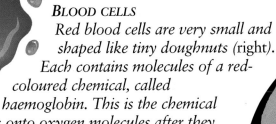

BLOOD CELLS
Red blood cells are very small and shaped like tiny doughnuts (right). Each contains molecules of a red-coloured chemical, called haemoglobin. This is the chemical that holds onto oxygen molecules after they are taken from the lungs. White blood cells vary in shape because they play a variety of roles when defending against infection (see pages 20-21).

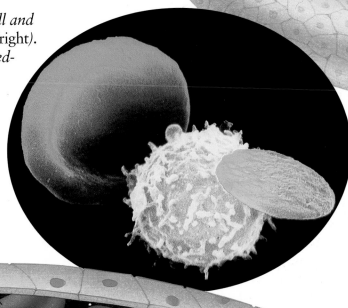

White blood cells

Platelets

Red blood cells

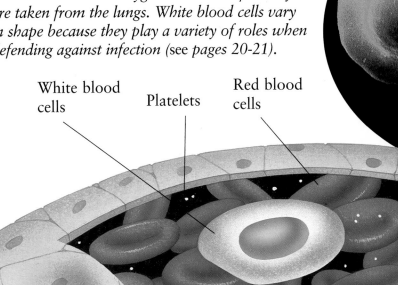

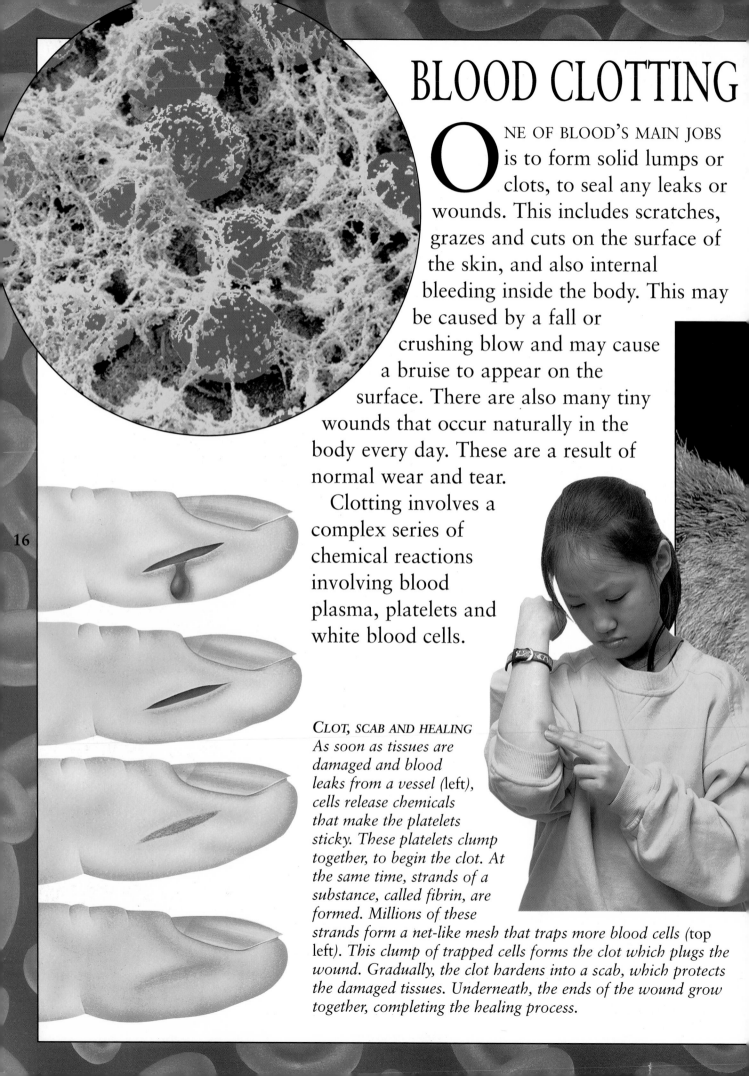

BLOOD CLOTTING

ONE OF BLOOD'S MAIN JOBS is to form solid lumps or clots, to seal any leaks or wounds. This includes scratches, grazes and cuts on the surface of the skin, and also internal bleeding inside the body. This may be caused by a fall or crushing blow and may cause a bruise to appear on the surface. There are also many tiny wounds that occur naturally in the body every day. These are a result of normal wear and tear.

Clotting involves a complex series of chemical reactions involving blood plasma, platelets and white blood cells.

CLOT, SCAB AND HEALING
As soon as tissues are damaged and blood leaks from a vessel (left), cells release chemicals that make the platelets sticky. These platelets clump together, to begin the clot. At the same time, strands of a substance, called fibrin, are formed. Millions of these strands form a net-like mesh that traps more blood cells (top left). This clump of trapped cells forms the clot which plugs the wound. Gradually, the clot hardens into a scab, which protects the damaged tissues. Underneath, the ends of the wound grow together, completing the healing process.

16

ANTI-CLOTTING

Some substances can prevent or slow down the formation of a blood clot. They are called anti-coagulants. Some blood-sucking animals, such as leeches, mosquitoes, fleas (right) and vampire bats (below), use them to keep the blood flowing freely as they feed on an animal.

Another group of substances, called thrombolytics, can make a fairly fresh blood clot loosen and disintegrate. They are often used as 'clot-busting' drugs in diseases such as heart attacks and strokes, where blood clots cause problems.

BLEEDING DISEASES

Haemophilia is an inherited condition that involves the lack of a blood-clotting chemical. Blood continues to leak from even a tiny wound. The condition nearly always affects males, but it can be passed on by unaffected female 'carriers'. Many of the European and Russian royal families of the 19th century (below) suffered from this condition.

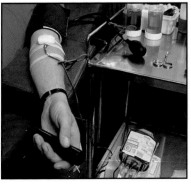

Donated blood must be treated carefully. Anti-clotting agents are sometimes added to ensure the blood does not clot once it has been taken out of the donor's body (left). Donated blood can be used in many ways, for treating patients in hospital (see page 14) and for emergency blood or fluid replacement.

DRAINING AWAY

BLOOD IS NOT the only fluid flowing around your body. There is another liquid which travels around its own system. This milky-white fluid is called lymph. The lymph system has vessels throughout the body as well as groups of nodes, which are sometimes called 'glands'. This system acts as the body's drain, taking away excess fluid from the body's cells. It also helps destroy germs and other foreign objects. Because the lymph system has no heart to push the fluid around, it relies on the movements of your body. These actions massage the fluid around the lymph system.

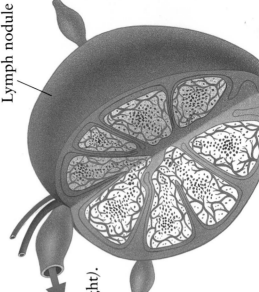

Lymph nodule

Valve

LYMPH NODES
The 'glands' in the neck, armpits, groin and other places, are called lymph nodes (right). These are lumps of lymph tissue, which contain millions of white blood cells. When you are ill, these white blood cells fight the germs causing the infection. This increase in activity causes the nodes to swell.

Adenoids

Tonsils

Vein

Among the best-known patches of lymph tissue are the tonsils (*below right*), on either side of the throat. They guard the entrance to the breathing passages and kill any airborne germs which land on them or nearby. The adenoids, at the back of the chamber inside the nose, do a similar job.

Sometimes the tonsils and adenoids remain swollen and very painful with infection. If this happens, they can be removed by surgery.

Adenoid

Tonsil

WHERE DOES LYMPH GO?

Lymph is made up of substances that are forced out of blood capillaries. It bathes the body's cells and then enters the lymph system through flaps in the lymph capillaries (below). Finally, it re-enters the blood through veins in the base of the neck (left).

Valves in the lymph vessels (above), like those in the veins (see page 12), make sure the lymph flows the correct way.

Lymph vessel

BODY CELLS

Lymph capillaries

Blood capillaries

FIGHTING INFECTION

BLOOD FORMS THE FRONT-LINE in the body's battle against infection. The white blood cells are the basis for this system. These cells patrol the body, fighting invading germs and cleaning the body's tissues of foreign substances and debris. They also try to destroy any of the body's own cells that become infected or have changed into cancer cells.

The largest white blood cells are called monocytes (above). These are three times the size of other kinds.

There are various kinds of white blood cells, each with a specific role in the body's defence. Some identify foreign bodies while others swallow and destroy them!

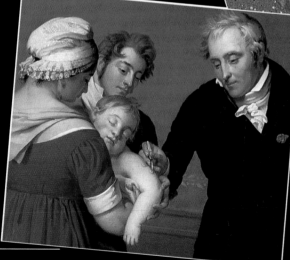

Macrophages (above) are scavenging white blood cells. They swallow germs, bits of debris and other foreign matter.

Doctors can protect your body against certain diseases, using a process called vaccination. This involves putting a specially weakened version of a disease into your body which stimulates the body's defences. After this, the body is protected, or immune. It can quickly 'recognise' the unweakened version of the disease if it infects you. It can then destroy the infection before it makes you ill. The first scientific tests on vaccinations were carried out by English physician Edward Jenner in 1796 (*above*).

SPECIAL IMPLANTS
Not all foreign objects are harmful to your body. Some can have beneficial roles, such as hip replacements (left). However, your body's defences don't always know this. If these implants were to start the defensive response, it could be disastrous. As a result, the surfaces of implants are made from materials that cannot stimulate your body's defences, such as stainless steel.

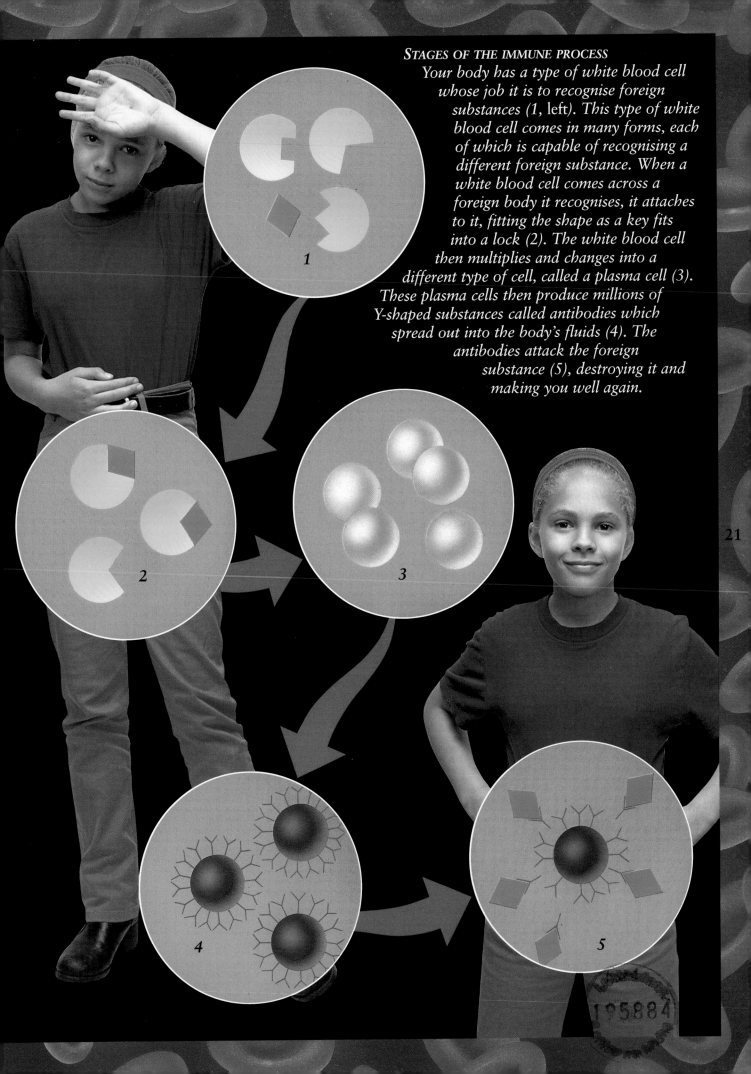

STAGES OF THE IMMUNE PROCESS

Your body has a type of white blood cell whose job it is to recognise foreign substances (1, left). This type of white blood cell comes in many forms, each of which is capable of recognising a different foreign substance. When a white blood cell comes across a foreign body it recognises, it attaches to it, fitting the shape as a key fits into a lock (2). The white blood cell then multiplies and changes into a different type of cell, called a plasma cell (3). These plasma cells then produce millions of Y-shaped substances called antibodies which spread out into the body's fluids (4). The antibodies attack the foreign substance (5), destroying it and making you well again.

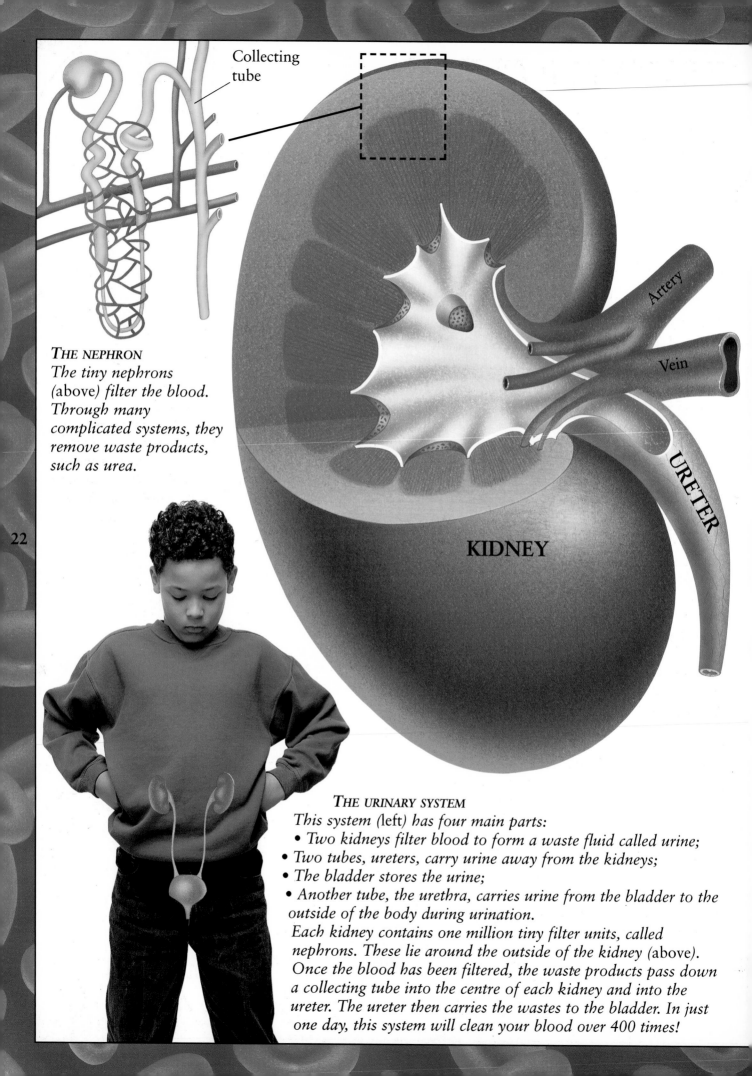

Collecting tube

THE NEPHRON
The tiny nephrons (above) filter the blood. Through many complicated systems, they remove waste products, such as urea.

Artery

Vein

URETER

KIDNEY

THE URINARY SYSTEM
This system (left) has four main parts:
• Two kidneys filter blood to form a waste fluid called urine;
• Two tubes, ureters, carry urine away from the kidneys;
• The bladder stores the urine;
• Another tube, the urethra, carries urine from the bladder to the outside of the body during urination.
Each kidney contains one million tiny filter units, called nephrons. These lie around the outside of the kidney (above). Once the blood has been filtered, the waste products pass down a collecting tube into the centre of each kidney and into the ureter. The ureter then carries the wastes to the bladder. In just one day, this system will clean your blood over 400 times!

KEEPING *it* CLEAN

AS A RESULT OF YOUR EVERYDAY ACTIVITIES, your body produces many waste products, especially carbon dioxide. These wastes seep into the blood and are carried away for removal, or excretion. There are two main systems for doing this – the lungs and the kidneys. The lungs get rid of carbon dioxide, while the kidneys filter out any excess salts and minerals and get rid of them through the bladder. However, this last process also removes a lot of water from your body, which needs to be replaced.

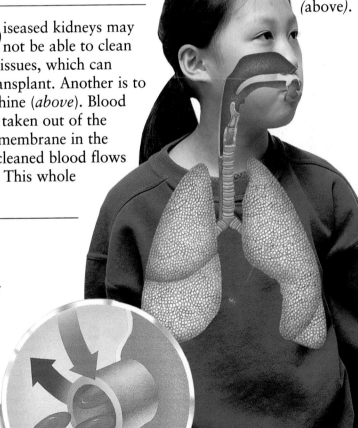

On average, the body loses at least 2 l (4 pints) of water every day. This liquid must be replaced by taking in water found in food and drink (above).

23

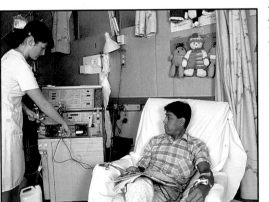

Diseased kidneys may not be able to clean the blood. Wastes build up in the blood and tissues, which can eventually be fatal. One option is a kidney transplant. Another is to filter the blood using an artificial kidney machine (*above*). Blood from a vessel, usually an artery in the arm, is taken out of the body along a plastic tube, to the machine. A membrane in the machine filters wastes out of the blood. The cleaned blood flows back along another tube into the body again. This whole process is called kidney dialysis.

REMOVING CARBON DIOXIDE
Once blood has taken oxygen to the body's cells, it collects the waste product of making energy, carbon dioxide. This is then taken to the lungs. Here the carbon dioxide seeps through the thin walls of the capillaries and into the lungs (below). At the same time it collects more supplies of oxygen to take to the cells. Your body gets rid of carbon dioxide simply by breathing out (right).

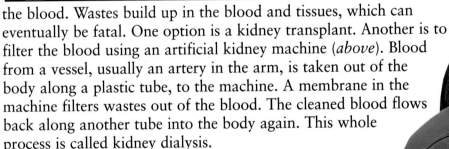

FOOD and BLOOD

Blood vessels

THE BILLIONS OF CELLS that make up your body need a constant supply of energy to ensure they can carry out all of their activities. These activities include multiplying, building new tissues and repairing damaged cells. The energy they need lies locked up in the food you eat. 'Unlocking' this energy requires the help of one of your body's largest organs – the liver. This 'chemical factory' processes nutrients so that your body's cells can use them. The liver also stores nutrients, recycles old body cells and breaks down harmful poisons that you might eat or drink.

RIGHT LOBE

Gall bladder

24

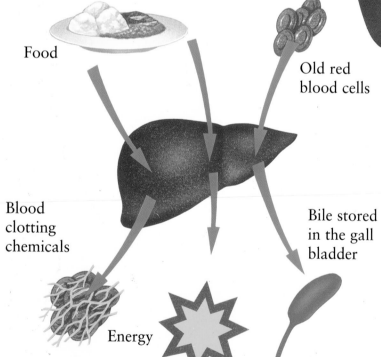

Food

Old red blood cells

Blood clotting chemicals

Bile stored in the gall bladder

Energy

ANY OLD IRON?
To ensure healthy blood, it is vital to eat foods rich in iron. This forms part of the haemoglobin found in red blood cells (see page 12). Good sources of iron are eggs and green vegetables (below). When red blood cells become old, they are broken down by the liver into bile, which is stored in the gall bladder (above). This chemical helps you digest fatty foods.

THE LIVER'S THREE MAIN ROLES
The liver has more than 300 chemical functions. These can be put into three main groups: it builds materials, such as the chemicals used in blood clotting; it stores substances, such as glucose, which is used to give energy; and it breaks down substances, such as red blood cells into bile (above).

LEFT
LOBE

TRANSPORT SYSTEM
Like a huge goods and marshalling yard in a railway network (right), the liver is a central part of the blood system. It sends fuel,
supplies and products to where they are needed. It also receives wastes and unwanted substances, which it re-routes for disposal.

Vein

Left lobe

Right lobe

Gall bladder

THE LIVER
The large, wedge-shaped liver lies just below the lungs in your chest. It has two parts, called lobes, the right lobe being much larger than the left (above). It also has a rich supply of blood which flows through the vessels inside the liver. This blood brings nutrients to give the liver energy, as well as food from the intestines to be processed (right).

25

Various harmful substances may be taken into the body by digestion. They include poisons in contaminated food, drugs or alcohol (*left*). The liver breaks down these substances to make them safe – a process called detoxification. If the liver is diseased it cannot detoxify the poisons. These can build up in the blood and may harm the body.

EXERCISE *and* BLOOD

LIKE MOST PARTS OF THE BODY, your heart and blood vessels become fitter and healthier if you exercise regularly. As you work harder, so the heart beats faster, forcing blood more quickly around your body. Also, the muscles in the arteries relax to make them wider (*see* page 12), helping the blood flow more easily. All of these help to meet the muscles' increased demand for oxygen and nutrients.

Without any form of regular activity that increases your heart rate, these parts of your blood system would become wasted and unhealthy.

HOW MUCH EXERCISE?
Human bodies are all different – so they need different amounts of exercise to stay healthy. A very general guide is to do three exercise sessions of 20-30 minutes each week. These should include activities that are hard enough to make the heart beat faster, breathing quicker and the skin slightly sweaty.

26

THE PROBLEM OF ALTITUDE
Air is thinner at high altitude. If a person is not used to high altitude, they may suffer from breathlessness. In extreme cases, such as the tops of the highest mountains, people need oxygen supplies to survive (above). This is because the body does not get enough oxygen to carry out its activities. However, after a few weeks at high altitude, the body adjusts by developing more red blood cells, increasing its ability to absorb oxygen.

Normal blood vessel

Dilated blood vessel

SWEATING AND FLUSHING

During exercise, muscles produce extra warmth. To avoid over-heating, the body gets rid of this by sweating and flushing. Sweat oozes onto the skin (right) and dries, drawing warmth from the body. Also, the blood vessels in the skin dilate, or become wider (left). This allows more warm blood to flow near the surface, where it can lose extra heat to the air around. This rush of blood also makes the skin look redder, or flushed.

Resting blood flow 1.2 l (2.5 pints) per minute

Active blood flow 12 l (25 pints) per minute

INCREASE THE FLOW

At rest, the heart pumps out over 5 l (10 pints) of blood per minute. During exercise, the heart beats faster, forcing out more blood each time. Your heart output can increase by up to five times. The amount of blood flowing to body parts also changes. When you are resting, such as when you are reading a book (left), the body's muscles receive about 1.2 l (2.5 pints) of blood per minute. During exercise, such as playing tennis, it can be as much as 12 l (25 pints) per minute.

27

Exercise has many beneficial effects on the body. The bones of the skeleton respond by becoming stronger, and joints move and bend more easily. Muscles become bigger and stronger, and have more capillaries to bring extra blood. This blood supplies them with extra nutrients and energy, and takes away waste products efficiently. The muscles become better able to cope with increased demand, without becoming stressed or injured.

BLOOD DISEASES

M ANY KINDS OF HEALTH PROBLEMS can affect the heart, blood vessels and blood. Some of these involve problems with the organs themselves. These are usually caused by the organs not developing properly or wear and tear to the system as it carries out its daily routine. Alternatively, foreign objects, such as bacteria and viruses, may attack the blood system. These can destroy cells, such as the white blood cells, leaving the body unprotected and open to attack from other illnesses.

LEUKAEMIAS
Leukaemias affect one or more of the types of white blood cells. In most types of leukaemia, the white cells become cancerous. They are unable to carry out their roles and multiply out of control. Treatments include various drugs, and a bone marrow transplant (above).

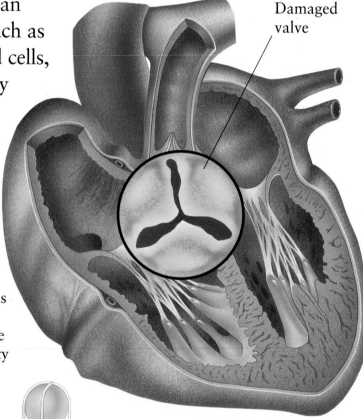

Damaged valve

T he illness anaemia is caused by a decline in the blood's ability to carry oxygen around the body. This creates fatigue, paleness and fainting. Anaemia may be caused by a diet lacking in iron, the essential part of haemoglobin, or from an inability to absorb the mineral. Alternatively, it may be caused by deformed red blood cells, such as sickle-cell anaemia. Here, the red cells are bent (*above*), and unable to carry oxygen as efficiently as normal red blood cells.

Open

Closed

HEART VALVE DISORDERS
Heart valves can become loose or frayed so that they do not close fully (above), allowing blood to flow the wrong way. They may also become stiff and unable to open fully. An infection of the valve's lining can also create a leak. Treatments include replacing the damaged valves with artificial valves (left), donated valves from humans or even valves from animals, such as pigs.

TREATING CORONARY DISEASE

If the blockage in a coronary artery (see page 8) is relatively small, it may be treated by a coronary angioplasty. A thin tube is threaded up through a blood vessel in the groin, to the heart and into the affected artery. Then a tiny balloon at the tip is inflated, to press against the blockage and open the artery. In the future, lasers may be used to blast away the blockage (right).

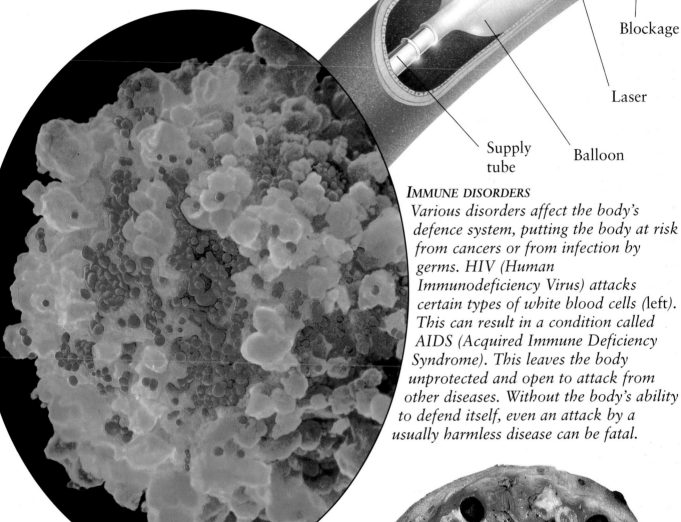

Blood vessel

Blockage

Laser

Supply tube

Balloon

IMMUNE DISORDERS

Various disorders affect the body's defence system, putting the body at risk from cancers or from infection by germs. HIV (Human Immunodeficiency Virus) attacks certain types of white blood cells (left). This can result in a condition called AIDS (Acquired Immune Deficiency Syndrome). This leaves the body unprotected and open to attack from other diseases. Without the body's ability to defend itself, even an attack by a usually harmless disease can be fatal.

29

PROTECTING THE HEART AND CIRCULATION

There are three main things we can do to keep the blood system healthy:
• Cut down on foods that have a high fat content, especially animal fats, such as cheese (right), which can form blockages in the arteries supplying blood to the heart's muscle (see page 8);
• Take plenty of regular exercise (see page 26-27);
• Do not smoke. Smoking can cause arteries to harden, depriving certain body parts of valuable nutrients and oxygen.

KNOW YOUR BODY!

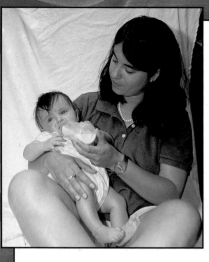

AS YOU GET OLDER, so the volume of blood inside you increases to meet the rising demands of your growing body. Newborn babies (left) will have about 0.25 l (0.5 pints) of blood. By the time they are fully grown they will have 5-6 l (10-12 pints) of blood if they are male, or 4-5 l (8-10 pints) if they are female.

IF ALL THE CAPILLARIES in an adult body were connected end to end, they would stretch for about 96,000 km (60,000 miles) – that's more than twice around the world (above)!

JUST ONE TEASPOON-FULL of blood contains, on average, 25 billion red blood cells (there are about 25 trillion in the whole body), 1.75 billion platelets and between 20-55 million white blood cells (right).

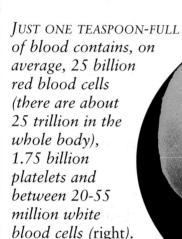

GIVING BLOOD (right) is very important, because blood is essential to replace fluids lost during an operation. During open-heart surgery in December 1970, fifty-year-old Warren C. Jyrich received an amazing 1,050 l (2,100 pints) of donated blood!

YOUR HEART (above) pumps, on average, 300 l (600 pints) of blood in one hour. This means it will push 7,200 l (14,400 pints) of blood into your arteries in a day, and a staggering 2.6 million l (5.2 million pints) of blood in a year.

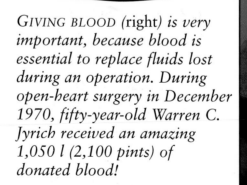

AT ANY ONE TIME, 64% of your blood (left) is flowing through your veins. A further 20% is pumping through the arteries and capillaries around your body, while another 9% is in the lungs. The final 7% is flowing through your brain.

GLOSSARY

Angiogram – An X-ray picture of a body part when special chemicals are injected to make sure the blood vessels can be seen.

Anti-coagulant – A chemical that prevents the blood from clotting. Doctors add it to donated blood to make it last longer.

Artery – A large blood vessel that carries blood away from the heart. It has a thick muscular wall because the blood flows through it at a very high pressure.

Atrium – The smaller upper chamber of the heart's pumping units. Blood enters the heart here before being pushed into the ventricle.

Bruise – A mark that appears on the skin. It is caused by damaged blood vessels beneath the surface.

Capillary – A tiny blood vessel that connects arteries to veins.

Fibrin – A substance which forms a net of tiny strands in the blood when you cut yourself. This net traps blood cells, forming a clot and plugs the wound.

Haemoglobin – The red-coloured chemical found in red blood cells. It holds on to oxygen to carry it around the body.

Heart – The organ that pushes blood around the blood vessels. It is found in the chest, sitting between the two lungs.

Pacemaker – An artificial device that controls the beating of the heart. It is placed beneath the skin of the shoulder and connected to the heart by wires.

Placenta – An organ found in the womb of a pregnant woman. It allows oxygen and nutrients to pass from the mother to the baby.

Plasma – The straw-coloured liquid which the blood cells float in. It is mostly made out of water, but does contain certain dissolved substances.

Platelet – A small fragment found in the blood that plays an important part during blood clotting.

Pulse – The rate at which your heart beats. The easiest place to feel your pulse is on the wrist.

Red blood cell – The doughnut-shaped cell that gives blood its red colour.

Scab – A solid lump of blood cells and fibres that forms when then skin and the underlying blood vessels have been cut.

Serum – The name given to blood plasma that has had its blood-clotting chemicals removed.

Umbilical cord – A tube which connects an unborn baby to the placenta. The baby's blood flows along this tube to collect oxygen and nutrients from the mother's blood.

Valve – A flap-like part of the blood system found in the heart and in some of the veins. These close to stop blood flowing the wrong way around the blood system.

Vein – A large blood vessel that carries blood back to the heart.

Ventricle – The larger of the chambers in the heart's pumping units. Each ventricle has thick muscular walls to force blood into the arteries at high pressure.

White blood cell – The white cells in the blood. Their job is to protect the body from foreign invaders, such as bacteria.

INDEX

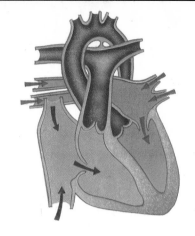

Photo credits: Abbreviations: t-top, m-middle, b-bottom, r-right, l-left

All the pictures in this book are by Science Photo Library except
the following pages:

4 & 25t – Spectrum Colour Library. 5 – Bruce Coleman
Collection. 7ml, 17m & 26 both – Frank Spooner Pictures.
17br – Hulton Getty Collection.

Additional photography by Roger Vlitos.